# The Art of Influence Simplified

How to Be a Trusted Advisor

Gregg Baron, CMC

*Success Sciences*

The Art of Influence Simplified

Printed by:
Success Sciences
www.Success-sciences.com

Copyright © 2016, Gregg Baron

Published in the United States of America

151005-00251

ISBN-13: 978- 0692587973
ISBN-10: 0692587977

For more information on Success Sciences call
(813) 989.9900 or go to www.success-sciences.com

# Here's What's Inside...

# Acknowledgment

Thank you to all of our clients over the years. We appreciate every opportunity to partner with you on making a "bigger difference" for your customers and team members. We consider it an honor to be a part of your quest for significant improvements in your team's ability to Earn and Retain MORE Successful Customer Relationships.

A heart felt thank you to the team at Success Sciences for everything they do every day. Jacqui Stiling, Bethmarie Fahey and Maria Sebti have provided exceptional support and assistance on this effort and many others. Their patience, persistence and superior support is valued and appreciated.

# Praise for the Approach

**Jeff Clarke**
CEO
Travel Impressions

At Travel Impressions our customers are our partners. The relationship is everything. The Art of Influence Simplified guides members of our sales team to always be looking for ways to personalize and enhance the customer experience, add value, and be easy to do business with. This approach provides the simple framework for consistently doing that well.

**Jeff Irmer**

Vice President, Global Sales & Commercial Excellence
Automation and Control Solutions
HONEYWELL INTERNATIONAL INC.

There are new rules in the sales world. The way people buy has significantly changed over time. Prospects and customers have access to an extraordinary amount of information. The Art of Influence Simplified amplifies the need to make the complex simple and proactively design customer experiences that enhance value, build confidence and trust.

**Fred Houston**
CEO
Columbia Ultimate

The difference this approach makes, beyond being effective, is how easy it is to learn, use and remember. The model makes the complex simple and that is the difference for sales professionals, support professionals and account managers actually using it.

**Rick Barrera**
Author of *Over Promise. Over Deliver*

Too many sales people are opportunity focused. The only thing they listen for is an opportunity for themselves! That leads to a selling disease with the symptoms of leaving opportunities on the table, not adding enough value, and not building an ongoing business relationship characterized by trust and respect. Far too many sales people have the disease because they are not taking the time to do what matters most when working to earn someone's business. The Art of Influence Simplified highlights what top professionals actually do to develop more and better sales results.

**Keith Lane**
VP Sales
Celebrity Cruises

There is nothing more useful than stepping into the other person's window and seeing the situation through their eyes. This approach has been working incredibly well for us in sales, coaching and leading. This model gives you a simple framework for approaching any situation when the objective is to influence effectively as well as enhance the relationship.

The unexpected surprise about The Art of Influence Simplified is that embedded in the model are a series of small things that open up into BIG insights that help you consistently influence others positively.

**Ben Milsom**
Chief Ticket Officer, Tampa Bay Buccaneers

What makes The Art of Influence Simplified particularly useful to me as a sales leader is its insightful, uncomplicated and gets right to what works.

**Tony Alessandra**
Author and CEO of Assessments 24X7

The buying experience has evolved dramatically. Unfortunately, sales practices haven't always kept up. The Art of Influence Simplified shows sales professionals how to close that gap by meeting customers and prospects where they are and flexing to what's important to them. It's simple, straight forward and the prescription for being much more effective in the current environment.

**Rich Vass**
Director Customer Relationships
eLearning Brothers

A model that is simple yet sophisticated, The Art of Influence Simplified clarifies elements of basic human interactions that - when combined - make all the difference in influencing outcomes during conversations.

**Jeff Berardo**
Regional Vice President
East Region at CIGNA Healthcare

As a sales leader who works with sales people every day, I have observed that one of the biggest differences between the great ones and the average ones is how much they stay focused on to the customer's perspective and priorities vs. working their own agenda. When building trust in a complex environment like healthcare it is critical to know your audience and exactly where you are adding value while keeping it as simple as possible. The Art of Influence Simplified cuts right to how to be more consistently effective at building and retaining more profitable relationships.

**Todd Cummings**
Director, Custom Courseware
eLearning Brothers Custom

The power of a model is its ability to simplify the complexity of life experiences. In The Art of Influence Simplified, what is simplified is the very complex and highly discussed area of relationships. Building relationships truly is an art. While the art of influence is truly not easy, this is a model that simplifies the complexity that allows anyone to confidently move forward to success.

**Pat Comunale**
President
Global Security Solutions Anixter

The Art of Influence Simplified adds a new level of ease that keeps sales and account management people focused on where to put their efforts to ensure ongoing effective customer relationships.

**Jim Micklos**
SVP, Business Development
Fusion Performance Marketing

Gregg Baron has hit pay dirt with the Art of Influence Simplified. Building trust is the foundation which makes influence possible. Utilizing Gregg's model leads to the desired results for your customers, your company and yourself!

**Bob Cestaro**
National Sales Director, Independent Distribution
Hussmann Corporation

The days of telling customers what your value proposition means to them are long gone. Successful salespeople today look at the world through their customer's eyes and realize that only the customer can determine value. The Art of Influence Simplified is a practical model that can help guide sellers in any industry to develop easy to understand solutions that are always aligned with the customer's definition of true value.

**Sheri Pasternak**
Senior Director, Field Sales
Travel Impressions

What is so powerful about The Art of Influence Simplified is its clarity and simplicity. In particular, making the invisible visible is both an incredibly valuable lesson and its "sticky" (you don't forget it).

# The Microbook Series

Success Sciences is a research based performance improvement firm. We focus on your team's ability to manage both the prospect and customer experience more consistently and successfully leading directly to enhanced sales and customer retention. Since 1986 we have worked with high profile clients that believe more successful customer relationships are a significant priority. With that shared priority we work collaboratively with our clients to design the strategies and practices that significantly impact the competence, confidence, and consistency of their sales and service professionals.

This series of Microbooks is an opportunity for us to share with you some of the core concepts that drive the success of our work. The purpose for the series and structuring it as Microbooks is to quickly share insights about core concepts and have you walk away with a heightened, updated, awareness of something you already knew or a new perspective that shifts your thinking forever.

In a world of information overload, we believe there is a need to be mindful of how we share the impactful information we provide. Each book is by design short enough to read on a single airline segment, giving you time to digest and then utilize the information quickly. It is not designed to be a comprehensive "how to" book. We can obviously dig a lot deeper into the topics and concepts in each book. For now, we want to challenge you to rethink the interpersonal aspects of how you do business. At a minimum, we would like you to look for those opportunities to incrementally change your approach to working with prospects and customers (or clients, members, subscribers, guests…) that will enhance your success and the success of your organization. Optimally, we want to challenge you to go bolder and stretch for something that can potentially be game changing for you and your organization.

If you are reading this book electronically you'll note several links to videos on the Success Sciences' website. Feel free to click to view as you read. If you are reading a paper copy of the book, please visit the links at your convenience. They will provide you with more information about some of the concepts we're discussing in the book.

Enjoy the series and let us know what you think. We would like to hear from you.

# Introduction to "The Art of Influence Simplified"

I've been doing this kind of work since the mid-80s. Some of the questions I get asked often are, "How do you really sell more effectively in this changing environment?" "How do you manage the customer's experience more consistently for a win-win?" "How do you go about persuading someone in a way that they feel really good about their interactions with you?" Those questions and most of the others I get asked come down to the Art of Influence.

I use questions extensively as a tool for inquiry and exploration as well as a primary tool for influence. In exploring the Art of Influence a few foundational questions include: What's the essence of positive influence? How do "the best of the best" influence? What specifically do elite sales people understand, believe, and consistently do to make them so good? Is it possible for anyone to take the essence of what consistently works well and use it across multiple business contexts?

This exploration of effective influence is primarily in the context of selling more effectively in Business to Business (B2B) situations. It is also effective in significant and or ongoing Business to Consumer (B2C) selling situations. Typically, this approach becomes less viable the more transactional the situation is. As part of the commitment to this being a Microbook and keeping the focus short and simple, we won't address the counter examples to using this model, or get into the broader applications including its value in enhancing leadership effectiveness.

Some of the insights and strategies of influencing that we will touch on have probably been around since the beginning of time. You may have come across them scattered in a variety of books, trainings and personal insights. The art of influencing people positively, whether it's in a formal sales context or informally selling your ideas is a requirement for success. What we set out to do in this short book is identify the underlying structure of what the "best of the best" believe and consistently do.

I hope it provides insights and ideas on how to better influence people positively and encourages you to put the mindset and practices in place to become a valued, sought-after, Trusted Advisor.

We are also inviting you to connect with us and explore what we aren't squeezing into this Microbook as part of our commitment to creating value for you and your sales team. Make notes, capture your thoughts and contact us about your situation.

Gregg Baron, CMC
Success Sciences Inc.
www.success-sciences.com

# The Vocabulary

**Influence** = Selling, leading, facilitating, persuading positively.

**Your Influence Outcome** = What you are selling, proposing or leading the other person to believe or do. It is the target of your influence effort.

**Customer** = Prospect, buyer (the person you are attempting to influence)

**Customer** = Client and all the variations (guest, member, subscriber…)

**ETDBW** = Easy To Do Business With

**Status Quo** = The existing state of affairs. How things are now.

**Shift** = Facilitate a change in perspective. Move others emotionally (change the way they feel).

**Perceive** = We want to point out that we use the word "see" throughout this work when we are discussing perception and perspectives. "See" is really a place holder for all modalities (see, hear and feel). We use the word 'see' throughout for simplicity and because 70% of the western world processes information visually. It is also a more natural link to our Windows on the World model.

**The Bones** = The underlying structure and mindset of our approach to influence. How we recommend you think about it vs. the tactics and skills for execution.

**The Meat** = The specific tactics, skills, practices and strategies of influence.

**Value** = What a person cares about, prioritizes or perceives as important. Value can take many forms including what they want to HAVE, DO, BE and/or FEEL

What is often over looked is that value is ultimately determined by how the person "feels". Value is always personal. Projecting or assuming what the other person values comes with risk. The way to minimize that risk is through working to get increasingly more committed and skilled at uncovering and utilizing the other person's perspective about what they value.

# Human Beings 101

## 3 Insights to carry throughout this reading

**FIRST:** A foundational insight that is often overlooked is that human beings are driven by one of two core possibilities in any given context. What drives human beings is either a) the desire to move toward payoffs, pleasure or benefits, or b) the need to move away from pain, fear, loss, embarrassment, or risk. Those core human drivers of moving toward payoffs and away from pain link directly to what individuals want (or do NOT want) to HAVE, DO, BE and/or FEEL. Facilitating what an individual wants to HAVE, DO, BE and/or FEEL creates value for them.

**SECOND:** No one ever changes their mind or behavior when they continue to see things the same way. All shifts in decisions and behavior are preceded by a shift in perception.

**THIRD:** Shifts in perception can trigger a shift in how people feel. How people feel is a powerful force in influencing decisions and behavior. Consider the shift from certainty to uncertainty; anxiety to confidence; no trust/ distrust to trust; feeling ignored to feeling acknowledged; not respected to respected; being taken for granted to feeling valued and appreciated.

> "Your greatest source of power is your ability to influence the way people *feel* and ultimately what they believe."

Our research in neuro economics, neuro linguistics, leadership effectiveness, sales effectiveness and observations across our culture indicate that this phrase articulates what just might be "the difference that makes the biggest difference" in being effective at influencing people positively.

These insights are fundamental to effective influence. Please keep them top of mind throughout.

# Why Don't More Sales People Influence More Positively and Effectively?

*"Too many sales people are opportunity focused. The only thing they listen for is an opportunity for themselves! That leads to a selling disease with the symptoms of leaving opportunities on the table, not adding enough value, and not building an ongoing business relationship characterized by trust and respect. Far too many sales people have the disease because they are not taking the time to do what matters most when working to earn someone's business. The Art of Influence Simplified highlights what top professionals actually do to develop more and better sales results."*

**Rick Barrera**
Author of *Over Promise. Over Deliver*

So, why don't more sales people influence more positively and effectively? In some situations, it's a lack of skillset. In more situations, it's about Mindset.

### *"Mindset before skillset to optimize execution"*

Some people are influencers by nature. They have a natural style and affinity for empathy, listening and putting others at ease. They are naturals at building credibility, authentic rapport and trust. Others are lucky to have great role models who also coach and guide them to become great influencers. However, in my experience, most of us aren't naturals at influencing effectively and have poor or nonexistent role models.

A good number of business people aren't getting the right quantity and quality of coaching, training and mentoring around this critical skill. Some don't get enough and some don't get any.

You've probably heard of Malcolm Gladwell the author of the *Tipping Point* and several other extraordinary books. In his book *Outliers*, Gladwell says that it takes roughly ten thousand hours of practice to achieve mastery in any field. That's a lot of practice. *The Art of Influence Simplified* hopes to save people a good chunk of those 10,000 hours by more quickly learning and understanding the patterns of what extraordinary influencers in business actually do.

Perhaps more importantly, is understanding what they believe. You will discover a few key beliefs of excellent influencers, perceived to be "Trusted Advisors" by their customers. If you are perceived as a Trusted Advisor vs the salesperson or worse, "the vendor" you are doing something different and that difference makes you more valuable and effective.

We could do multiple books on why a significant percentage of salespeople don't influence as positively or as effectively as they could. A short list begins with:

- They prioritize their self-interest over the customer / prospect

- They don't work on their craft (Professional Influence) at all or enough

- They don't listen effectively on all levels

- They don't prepare effectively

- They pitch too much
- They don't customize their approach at all or enough for each unique customer
- They don't effectively establish credibility which impacts trust, which impacts everything
- They don't have the will or the skill to uncover the value the customer wants (what they really care about, prioritize, want and need)
- They speak their own language and don't learn and speak the prospect's language
- They aren't ETDBW (Easy To Do Business With)
- They don't make the sales experience valuable enough for the customer

Value Creation (Their Perspective)
Their Experience (Their Perspective)

Manage
Anxiety and
Confidence
(trust)

Your
Influence
Outcome

Make the
Invisible
Visible
(shift)

Make the
Complex
Simple
(ease)

TM

## The Model from 50,000 ft

When looking at this model as a whole you will notice that there are six integrated focal points. The focal points are overlapping and circular vs. separate and linear. Each represents significant insights to guide your strategy for influencing positively and positioning you for potentially being perceived as a Trusted Advisor.

The goal of the model and this Microbook is to act as a guide for how to think about influence. We call that the "BARE BONES." The other part of the work is the "MEAT" on the bones. That includes all the specific strategies, practices and skill sets that you can use to execute this approach to positive influence. The "MEAT" on the bones will get a relatively brief mention in this short book given our stated purpose and use of the Microbook format.

## "Mindset before skillset to optimize execution"

We recommend you don't get distracted by the "how to" tactics before you get the whole view of the approach and the essence of the philosophy. A solid foundation of the bare bones and beliefs that support the approach will ultimately take your influence effectiveness further and faster. It will also serve you in more effectively planning your influence efforts in most business situations.

Once you have the core insights, the view of the model (and how it fits together) will become more significant and valuable to you. There are several skill sets, some of which we will address and some of which we will simply reference before digging into the middle of the model. Those we will address include Windows on the World (different perspectives), Syncing Up™ (rapport building model), Strategic Listening and Asking Exploring Questions. They may all sound like obvious skills, however consistent, effective and strategic execution of the obvious has proven to be less common with many people who sell every day. Understanding the importance of these skills will enable you to better understand the mindset and philosophy behind *The Art of Influence Simplified*.

At the center of the model is your Influence Outcome(s). We understand that if you are a Sales Professional you have a job to do with clear objectives that you need to accomplish. We understand that and caution you about your objectives possibly dominating your mindset. We share that in the context of you wanting to be effective long term and you seeing the advantages in truly becoming a Trusted Advisor. Consider this obvious statement:

Achieving Your Influence Outcome (your desire for what you would like the buyer to believe and/or do) can be more positively and effectively facilitated when you successfully create value for the buyer.

The purpose here is to not waste your time sharing the remedial or obvious. It is pointing out the gap between what sales people often know, contrasted with what the research says they too infrequently do.

We are suggesting that the root of this knowing / doing gap is mindset, not ignorance. The research points out buyers are choosing to work with Sales Professionals that deliver more value to them in the sales process than their competitors. It is a major part of the story of who earns the business and who doesn't. It's an even bigger part of the story of who wins when it comes to the longer-term payoffs of customer loyalty and retention.

That makes us wonder why the number of sales people that dial into what actually creates value for their buyers isn't much higher. We are convinced that the answer is mindset.

# 6 Focal Points of the Model

You will be using each of these to guide your thinking:

1. **Value Creation** (from <u>their</u> perspective)

2. **Managing their <u>experience</u>** (on every level, at all times to be perceived as valuable by <u>them)</u>

3. Effectively **Managing their Anxiety and Confidence** (as part of managing the way they *feel*)

4. **Making the Complex Simple** (and the difficult easy) for <u>them</u>

5. **Making the Invisible Visible** (so they can distinctly see what they need to see to trigger a shift in perception and behavior)

6. **Your Influence Outcome** (what you want the other person to understand, believe and/or do)

All 6 focal points of the model are often happening simultaneously. It may be easier to visualize the 6 focal points by thinking about a technology that came out in the mid1980s, called Picture in Picture, or PiP. Picture in Picture technology allows you to see one picture on your television screen while viewing an additional channel in a smaller picture simultaneously. This enables the viewer to keep their eyes on both programs at once. PiP works much the same in *The Art of Influence Simplified*

*Model.* The 6 focal points of the model need to remain on your "screen". Depending on where you are in the process, you may magnify one of the focal points without taking your eyes off the rest of them.

## Focal Point #1 (Value Creation)

Starting with the outer circle of the model, the design is aimed at focusing you on the <u>mindset</u> you should ideally have in all of your planning, conversations and follow up. It is where your focus should start and remain throughout. **Notice how everything else in the model is contained within the mindset of creating value for <u>them</u> including Your Influence Outcome.** When the goal is ultimately developing, sustaining and / or enhancing a relationship that is ongoing and positive, you need to deliver *notable* value. To the extent that you do that well, the possibility of becoming a Trusted Advisor will be enhanced.

## Have Do Be Feel

We think about creating value for others as anything that will enable them to HAVE, DO, BE or FEEL what they care about in any combination. That would include anything that may have been previously out of their awareness or invisible.

HAVE DO BE FEEL™

This invisible value can exist for a few reasons. They may have a preconceived idea of the solution based on limited information, past experiences or biases that block or limit their view of the possible. They don't have the depth of expertise and experience in your solutions therefore they can't see what you see.

Asking high quality, appropriate questions that properly probe and help clarify often allows the customer to discover wants, needs or possibilities that were previously off their radar. When you facilitate this process well you are likely creating value for the other person when they discover what was previously foggy or invisible.

Think of an iceberg. Above the water line are the more obvious conditions, needs, preferences and

expectations. Below the waterline are unknowns. Unknowns have the potential for being the most important things to be aware of.

Using research of all kinds, and using Exploring Questions and Strategic Listening takes us below the water line allowing both the customer and us to see what is potentially valuable or important. All of which ultimately comes down to some version of what the customer wants to HAVE, DO, BE and/or FEEL.

A few examples for BE and FEEL: (HAVE and DO are limitless and more obvious.)

- BE – What they want to BE relates to their identity and aspirations. Examples - A risk taker, leader, innovator, builder, explorer, problem-solver, winner, credible or expert are a few descriptions of ways of being...

- FEEL – Examples include: appreciated, respected, valued, comfortable, courageous, trustworthy, trusted, relief, secure, confident, clear, safe, capable, smart (right), happy, excited, clever, admired, like they got a good deal, like they are making progress...

Ask yourself - what can you contribute to what they want to HAVE, DO, BE and/or FEEL? How can you position where you are leading them to enhance or preserve what they want to HAVE, DO, BE and/or FEEL?

You have the best opportunity to positively influence people and become a Trusted Advisor when your mindset is about creating value for the other person and seeing the situation and context from their perspective. We all know that value is very personal and what has value for one person may not for another. We all know that, yet so many sales people approach influencing people in the same way, for everyone.

**Caution** - If your efforts are perceived to be a touch too much about your agenda, what you want, need or value, you're going in the wrong direction and will miss the longer term opportunity (and very likely the short term opportunity). Think, focus and act in alignment with creating value from <u>their</u> perspective not yours.

**Caution** - As you look for opportunities above and below the surface to create value for those you are influencing, don't get derailed by too quickly jumping in with solutions and possibilities. Be a problem finder, need finder and value clarifier. Resist the urge to "sound brilliant" by jumping in too quickly and telling, proposing and pitching before you have worked to uncover what may be invisible.

A summary of a few things you want to discover as you work with your customer or prospect:

- What do <u>they</u> care about? What matters more? What matters most to them?

- What do they most want to HAVE, DO, BE and/or FEEL?

- What issues, challenges and/or risks are they trying to solve, minimize or avoid?

- What are their priorities or would be if they had access to your perspective and experience?

- What advantages, capabilities or benefits do they seek and prioritize?

- If you stop assuming and projecting what creates value for them, what might you learn about what could make the biggest difference in them making a shift?

Having the right mindset makes a dramatic difference in your ability to breakthrough in this area. Previously, we cautioned you about allowing <u>your</u> objectives to dominate your mindset. You may have a paradigm that is keeping you from seeing how much you are driven by your objectives and/ or how much assuming and projecting you actually do with your prospects.

Know that you may even have the "right intentions". Mindset and intentions aren't always aligned. Consider your last several attempts at dieting. Chances are you had good intentions. What is important for you to realize is *your intentions take a distant second place to customer perceptions when it comes to influence.* Think about Value Creation from their perspective.

# Focal Point #2 (Managing Their Experience from Their Perspective)

When we refer to Their Experience (from their perspective) we mean the Prospect Experience or Sales Experience they have with you when you are attempting to influence them. That would include:

- Sales meetings
- Phone calls
- Correspondence
- How responsive you are
- How reliable you are
- How prepared you are
- How knowledgeable and insightful you are
- How well you manage expectations and perceptions
- How you communicate

**Essentially everything attached to what they experience in the process.**

The experience they have is part of the Value Creation focal point in the model. It is also a distinct focal point on its own and deceptively important to your success in both earning the business and being positioned to be a Trusted Advisor that retains and expands the business.

Various pieces of research have shown that the experience a buyer has in the B2B sales process will be the dominant factor in the decision of who they choose to go with _and_ will also impact their loyalty.

Your company and brand reputation, product/service delivery, value to price ratio and similar considerations are clearly very important. However, in B2B sales situations the _perceived value of the sales experience to the buyer is the biggest factor in not only earning the business it is significantly impactful downstream when it comes to retaining and expanding the business they do with you._

(Please contact us if you would like to explore the specifics about the research and how to use it with your sales team.)

www.success-sciences.com/AboutUs/ContactUs/ContactUs.htm

# Windows on the World

You now have heightened awareness of how critical it is to focus on value creation for the person you are influencing. Note that we will continue to beat this dead horse through the rest of this Microbook as part of our dedication to shifting your mindset. To prove it we are going to introduce a model to help you visualize how to do this more specifically and effectively.

Effective influence begins with your willingness and ability to understand the other person. Steven Covey may have said it best and most simply as Habit number 5 of his 7 Habits – "Seek first to understand, then to be understood." In our training programs, we emphasize that point, and coach participants to see the situation from the buyer's perspective before pitching, selling and telling from their own perspective.

What we are talking about here sounds obvious to most everyone reading this. Most sales people know and understand what we are advocating. We are hitting the point hard because we have consistently observed this as another big Knowing /Doing gap in sales performance. Sales people know this yet we consistently observe them not putting it in practice.

## Different Perspectives

The Windows on the World model can help us understand why different people react differently to the same situation. It shows graphically, how we each respond to people, situations, opportunities, challenges and events, based on our view of them.

Since our points of view are not the same, neither are our responses. Our perspective about a situation or a person is filtered by the panes in our window. These panes or filters are our expectations, experiences, needs and most importantly our beliefs.

*"To understand people, understand how they see the world."*

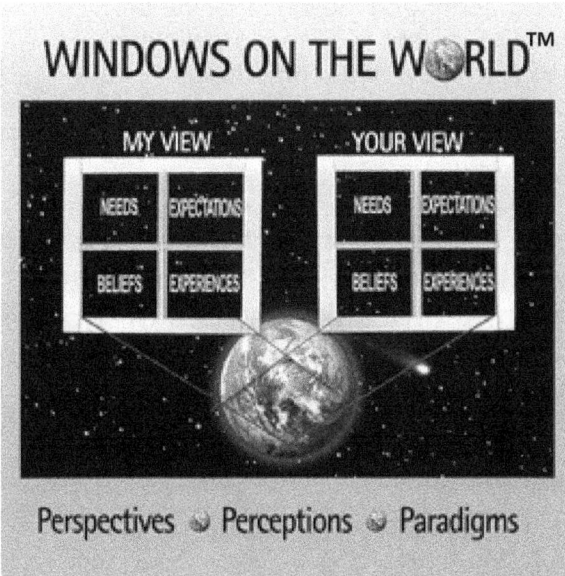

WINDOWS ON THE WORLD™

MY VIEW          YOUR VIEW

NEEDS  EXPECTATIONS          NEEDS  EXPECTATIONS

BELIEFS  EXPERIENCES          BELIEFS  EXPERIENCES

Perspectives ☺ Perceptions ☺ Paradigms

*"Your perspective informs your perception and your perception is your reality."*

When most people look at a chunk of marble, they typically see a rock. When a sculptor looks at that same piece of marble, she sees the statue it could become. The piece of marble is the same, but the perspective of it is very different.

We all know that in many sales situations the prospect has an initial view or perspective that is different than ours. We have information, experiences and expertise that they don't have. And they have beliefs, expectations, experiences, needs, information, and feelings that we aren't initially (or ever) aware of. The more we can understand their view and them, the higher the probability we will be able to help them see how where we are leading them will benefit them.

---

**Coaching Point – See the issue or opportunity through the eyes of those you serve.**

---

### Facilitating the Shift

Think about every time you've made a decision, changed your behavior, changed direction, took on a new approach. Something happened to trigger that change. For some reason you "saw" that situation in a new light. Something about your perspective changed. The view from your window shifted, which impacted your perception and your perception is your reality.

An effective influencer facilitates that shift. They create the conditions that pivot the focus from the customer's window to their window.

A non-business example is a friend of mine who was a lifetime smoker. She started in her teens and had no intention of quitting. She knew all the statistics and health risks. She knew people who had died of lung cancer. None of this had any impact on her desire to quit. Until her son and daughter-in-law announced they were expecting their first child. Suddenly the world shifted and the thought of her new grandbaby seeing his grandmother die of lung cancer was the trigger that changed her behavior. She had a brief vision of herself through her grandchild's eyes and didn't like the view.

When a person's perspective stays the same, they will default to the status quo (stay with the current choice/behavior /decision/ approach/ product/service/ supplier/ solution).

Effective Influence is the ability to facilitate the other person's willingness to see a "distinct perspective" because:

"Human Beings never change their behavior when they continue to see things from the same perspective."

## Syncing Up™

What we have discovered so far is particularly important.

1. Value Creation is the primary mindset to support you in becoming a Trusted Advisor and effective influencer.

2. One key to Value Creation is managing the experience the customer has with you. That experience needs to be perceived as high value to <u>them</u>.

The Windows section provided insight and direction on how to tap into their perspective and what creates value for them. This section on Syncing Up™ will provide a few insights for managing their experience and positively influencing the way they *feel*.

If you think about the things that have impacted the way you have felt in a variety of situations you will notice that they can have a dramatic impact on your decisions, behavior and relationships.

> *"I've learned that people will forget what you said, people will forget what you did, but people will never forget how you made them feel."*
>
> ~Maya Angelou

Gaining influence comes with behaviorally adjusting to the customer /prospect. We call the skillset to make those adjustments Syncing Up™. It's paying very close attention to two key distinctions and making the appropriate adjustments in your approach based on specific things you hear and observe.

Syncing Up™ is about building genuine rapport, which is not small talk. In our sales, service, leadership, coaching and influence trainings we use a four quadrant behavioral model (Syncing Up™) that is easy to learn, use and remember.

The success of the approach begins with how easy it is to identify a predictable pattern of behaviors based on two continuums. The first is pace (faster or slower) and the second is priority (people vs. task).

It's a fast track to knowing what to adjust in your communication. It will guide you in how to make those adjustments that lead to your prospect FEELING more comfortable with you. They feel more comfortable because you are moving at their pace and perceive that you share a similar focus when it comes to relationship and task.

There are many models out there that range in complexity and usability. You've probably been exposed to at least one if not more. The key is to make use of this knowledge to more quickly reach a level of rapport that is comfortable for the other person. When you do the experience is comfortable for them. When you don't, it leads to them FEELING less than comfortable with you when your natural styles don't have enough alignment.

This approach actually touches all three of the inner circles in the model and the outer circle of "Their Experience". When executed well Syncing Up™ unquestionably helps you manage their anxiety and confidence. It also will aid in your efforts to make the complex simple and the difficult easy. When you package and present yourself (including your communication) to more closely match the way they prefer to receive and process information, they respond better.

Skilled influencers also adjust their approach to asking questions by style. Asking questions is the primary method for making the invisible, visible.

Overall, knowing what their behavioral style is helps you make multiple distinctions about who they are, what they value, how they think, process information and make decisions. Your efforts to master Syncing Up™ will speed your efforts to seeing many invisible characteristics, tendencies and preferences in yourself and other people.

A timeless sales phrase is: no trust, no sale. When you can establish trust by design, manage their confidence in you and how it *feels* to interact with you, you are proactively managing a key part of their experience. Syncing Up™ will make a

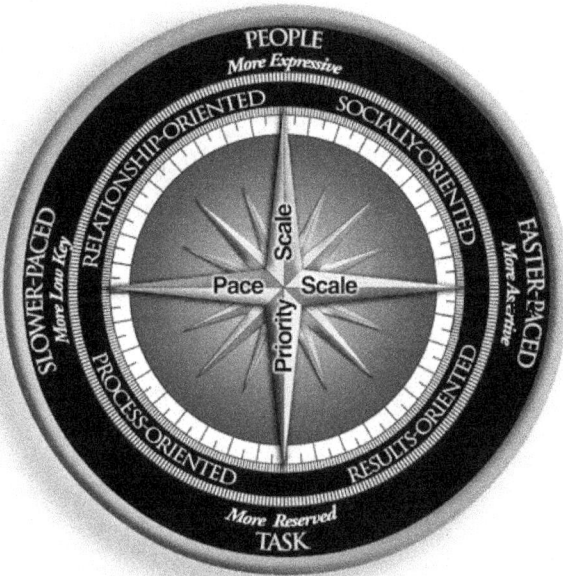

surprisingly quick and significant difference in your ability to establish authentic rapport and trust. It will definitely help you influence the other person to look through your window and see a new perspective.

There are books, videos, and trainings on four quadrant models like Syncing Up™. Please contact us for options.

www.success-sciences.com/ServiceEnhancementGroup/Syncing Up/Syncing-Up.htm

# Art of Influence Simplified

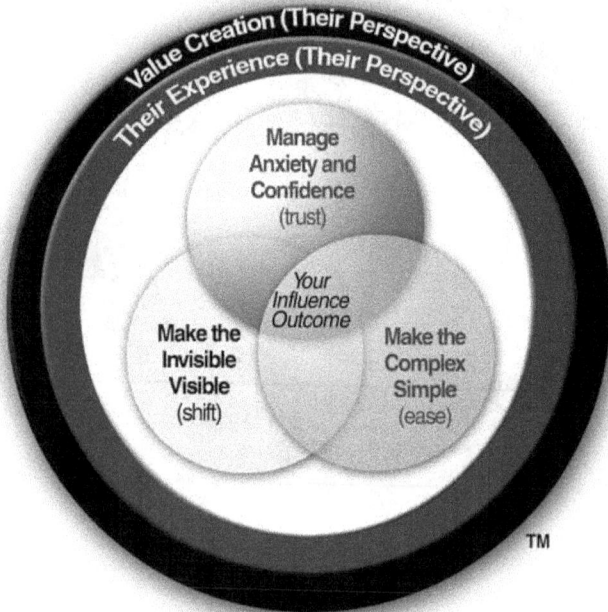

It's time to shift our focus from all the context we have created and get more familiar with the inner circles of the model.

## Focal Points #3 - #5

As you look at the model you see there are three overlapping circles. In the overlap is Your Influence Outcome. The way to increase the probability of achieving Your Influence Outcome is by effectively executing in each of the three circles to positively change the way the person *feels* and create value in the experience:

- Manage anxiety and confidence (trust)

- Make the complex simple (ease)

- Make the invisible visible (shift)

These are significant approaches to managing their overall experience and are the right ingredients to create the conditions for influence.

Effectively managing the other person's confidence in you, your organization, and what you are proposing (directly or indirectly) is clearly part of achieving positive influence.

The general guidelines for doing this include proactively managing perceptions and expectations on every level as you continue to listen and Sync Up™. When you encounter any hint of anxiety or concern from the prospect you need to "step into it," not over it. Remember the iceberg analogy from earlier? Anything left hidden can be potentially dangerous to achieving Your Influence Outcome. Better to bring it out into the open and deal with it instead of letting it fester and kill your Trusted Advisor potential.

Earlier we talked about what the other person wants to HAVE, DO, BE and/or FEEL. Not only is this an important consideration for how we frame any potential solution, it is also important to manage anxiety, increase confidence and influence. If we know and understand what the other person wants to HAVE, DO, BE and/or FEEL (and what they don't) we know what to emphasize and what to avoid.

**Your greatest source of power is in your ability to influence the way people *feel* (by guiding what they perceive) to ultimately influence what they believe.**

We come back to this over and over again because it's core to being a Trusted Advisor. It makes a very big difference in being effective.

## Manage Anxiety & Confidence

What is your reputation going into the conversation? Do you have credibility?

For example, did someone the prospect trusts and respects refer you? Do you have credibility in your role? What would someone perceive if they did a little digital research about you? Your company? Your solutions? Checked your references the old fashioned way?

We have come across some research that indicates that people who only talk about what is "positive, wonderful and beautiful" have less credibility than people who also include something that is less than perfect. (It doesn't have to be significant, it can be something relatively small). The other person's confidence in you and your credibility increases when you acknowledge the less than perfect. It speaks to your authenticity to reveal some level of vulnerability.

How do people perceive you after a conversation? Do they perceive you as authentic, straightforward and direct? Or do they hear a politician dancing around their question? Are you able to consistently communicate in a way that increases your credibility?

You can be proactive in your efforts to establish credibility. For example, do you share stories and case studies about the value you create using the words of current or past customer's? Do you utilize 3$^{rd}$ party proof statements or evidence that supports your claims, credibility and trustworthiness?

**Coaching Point -** The key to managing anxiety and confidence is managing perceptions and expectations. Really listening to the content, context, and emotions of the other person is foundational to managing their perceptions and expectations.

Acknowledging the other person's needs and expectations goes a long way. People feel more confident in you when they feel validated.

# Make the Complex Simple

*"Not everyone needs to know how to build a watch to be able to tell time"*

The next focal point is making the complex simple for the person you are influencing. We live in complex times. We are bombarded daily with information, ideas, instructions and other minutia. Everything and everyone talks to us – our cars, smart phones, tablets, TVs, podcasts, co-workers, customers, family and on and on.

We live in a world of information overload. The last thing our customers need is more information than required to digest, decipher and decode. Individuals will reach a point where more information and/or more complex processes just *feels* like more work.

**More work than value = a problem.**

Saving someone time, effort and hassle creates value for them. It makes their experience more valuable when there is less effort for them (on every level) and appropriate simplicity.

Most of us crave simplicity. The request that is typically unstated is: *Help me understand in a way that is useful to me and not just more noise. I already have too much noise and blur in my world.*

Let's play with this: what's the best word to describe the opposite of simplify? Visualize a continuum with simplify on one end. What would you write on the opposite end? I'd write "complexify".

I offer that word with a bit of grin. People who know a little about grammar will say complexify is not a word, and they are right. Spellcheck rejects complexify every time. But, there is nothing better to articulate the opposite of simplify than complexify. Anyone who has assembled a piece of furniture from Ikea knows the difference between simplify and complexify.

## COMPLEXIFY ™

## SIMPLIFY

The box that says "simple assembly required" usually means hours of agonizing over pages of directions, written in multiple languages with confusing images, to complete the "simple" assembly. That type of experience "changes the way you FEEL." Many of us would say it is more value subtracting than value adding.

Human Beings 101 - People "move toward" what they perceive to be appropriately simple, easy and understandable and "move away" from anxiety, complexity and unnecessary work/effort. Your job as the Sales Professional is to take what might look and feel to them as complex and appropriately simplify it.

Everyone is different. Consider their Syncing Up™ behavioral style. Your goal is to find the **Goldilocks Zone**. Not too simple. Not too complex. The way to do that for each unique individual, is by looking through their window and then adjusting to them.

It's fair to say that most of us are already near the saturation point of information overload. Product knowledge dumps, more often than not, produce unintended anxiety. Ask yourself:

- What does the customer really need (want and prefer) to know now?

- How can I share the information in a way that is manageable for them?

- How can I break this down to the chunk size and level of sophistication that meets this person where they are vs. what is easy for me to share?

- Ask yourself - Am I about to explain the root system when all they want is the fruit?

A colleague of mine tells a story about a time very early in her sales career. She was selling corporate wellness programs and had what seemed to be a very productive meeting with the owner of a small business. She was getting all green lights and thinking she had the sale. She began to tell him very enthusiastically about all of the different options for implementing the program. As she went on the business owner began to look more and more anxious. When she paused for a breath he politely said he had to think it over more and would call her later. When she followed up she was told he decided not to go with the program. When she probed about why, he confessed that "it just seemed too complex, there were too many options." A lesson she never forgot.

Looking through their window, Strategic Listening and Syncing Up™ will get you more success than the "one size fits all" pitch. Think baseball - A pitch is one direction and irreversible.

Think sales - A standard pitch is the hope that your guesses about what you are throwing at the prospect will appeal to that person. Typically, a standard pitch is a low probability approach for ultimately establishing a relationship with someone as their Trusted Advisor. The powerful forces of the unique needs, expectations, experiences and beliefs of that INDIVIDIDUAL have to be a lucky match to your hopeful guess. Consider this: A standard pitch is typically driven by your needs and agenda not theirs.

Part of our role as Sales Professionals is to *make the complex simple and the difficult easy* for prospects and customers. When you do, it positively changes the way they *feel* and adds value to their experience. When you do this poorly (or not as well as your competitors) they notice and it hurts your efforts to win the business.

In every way and on every level, be ETDBW. The perspective about what is complex, easy or difficult must be theirs and NOT yours. Calibrate everything, don't assume or project from your window.

# Make the Invisible Visible

This focal point is something that we've mentioned multiple times and will do a short recap here to emphasize what's most important.

The two big takeaways are – "No one changes their mind or behavior when they continue to see things the same way." Any shift in behavior is preceded by a shift in perspective which shifts perception(s). To make that happen your job is to facilitate making what is invisible to them, visible.

Second: To shift a customer's perspective effectively, you need to understand their expectations, experiences, needs and beliefs. These might initially be invisible to you, and you will need to make the effort to see what you initially can't. Once you uncover what needs to be visible to you, you will optimize your ability in finding what needs to be visible to them.

# Playing Sales Jazz™

As you become increasingly sophisticated at influencing you discover the craft is part science and part art. One of my favorite forms of art is jazz.

What makes jazz different from almost any other kind of music? Improvisation. One of the most important things you can do to enhance your success in any situation is thinking in advance. That means planning, anticipating, practicing and being more strategic.

If you were a professional jazz musician you would work on your craft. You would practice, rehearse, listen and watch your performances in an effort to get better and be prepared for your next performance. However, as a jazz musician, when you get into the performance, you must be able to improvise.

The same is true for a Sales Professional. You plan, anticipate and prepare before the sales call. Then you adjust and flex in the moment based on what you're learning, hearing, seeing, and gathering as you are engaging with the customer.

The recommendation is to "always go in with a plan, and expect to improvise." This approach is called Sales Jazz™. It addresses the real world need to remain focused and flexible throughout the process. That includes syncing to their behavioral style, adjusting the type of questions you ask and *how* you ask them, the time you have for the conversation, the solution path you intended to go down and essentially everything else.

We see extraordinary sales professionals:

1. Anticipate, prepare and start the sales call with a clear plan

2. Improvise, flex, adapt and adjust as the invisible becomes visible

3. Remain focused, balanced and adaptable throughout the process to optimally manage the value of the experience for the customer

The plan should typically start with Your Influence Outcome (what you want them to understand, believe and/or do) in this next step and overall. Then formulate your plan to include anything you already know about their behavioral style, expectations, experiences, needs, beliefs, priorities, preferences and history.

**Coaching Point** - Go into every sales situation prepared and with a clear plan. Then be in the moment by listening strategically and improvise as needed to enhance the experience and the value you deliver for your audience.

# The Art of Influence Works in Many Different Sales Environments

We've been helping sales teams positively influence people since 1986 with very diverse high profile clients. We've worked a lot in the travel industry. A major cruise line client went from 68,000 confirmed bookings in the baseline year to 149,000 confirmed bookings with the same head count and no additional investments in technology. We helped their people think differently and approach each conversation with many of the insights we have shared here.

The reason they were able to increase their bookings so significantly was we taught them the mindset and skillset for becoming Trusted Advisors.

The key for this client was managing the conversation (the sales experience) to be focused on discovering what the prospect (guest) cared about through listening and facilitating vs. taking an order or pitching. We put a lot of emphasis on managing the sales experience. The key to managing the sales experience was developing competence and confidence in using Syncing Up™, asking Exploring questions, Strategic Listening, managing anxiety and confidence and making the invisible visible.

We also work with a major insurance company who is on the high end of the cost spectrum compared to their competitors. We were able to help them approach the sales process differently. Instead of the usual pitching we taught them how to be Trusted Advisors and be more strategic by stepping back and doing the right amount of pre-call planning.

We helped them facilitate the key shift in perspective for the end user clients and brokers only "seeing" the price to "seeing" a distinct perspective about the cost of poor healthcare and the invisible payoffs and advantages of wellness.

The summary of major distinctions in this case study:

**1) Making the complex simple – and the difficult easy.**

The Affordable Care Act and all of the dramatic changes in healthcare begged for someone to simplify the changes, options and possibilities. Someone needed to make the process MUCH EASIER to understand and navigate.

This simplification alone positively changed the way clients and brokers felt not only about what was being proposed, but also about their account managers and sales people. The credible professionals who delivered the high value experience through simplifying and navigating all the pitfalls were perceived as difference makers.

**2) Making the Invisible Visible**

What needed to happen was a reframe of the traditional focus from the price of the premium to the hidden value and payoffs that were invisible. Clients and brokers needed to see the only sustainable way to control the cost of healthcare is through disease prevention and health improvement.

The credibility of the reframe came from being able to prove the hidden benefits through 3rd party research from sources such as the Federal Government.

We have many case studies across multiple, diverse industries and contexts. We would be happy to share relevant case studies with you so you can see the applications to your situation.

# This Was Only the Bare Bones

We mentioned in the beginning that this Microbook was intended to only give you the "bare bones" of Influence. It was not a comprehensive how to. It's a way of thinking about the influence process and how to increase the probability of your success.

Think of what we shared here as the underlying structure to guide all of the possible skills, tactics and practices for effective influence that lead to you being a Trusted Advisor. When it comes to the actual execution of this approach we put some "meat" on those bones. That's when we get deeply into skillsets such as:

- Pre-call planning
- Differentiating you, your organization, the experience they have with you and your offer
- Designing and asking highly effective open-ended exploring questions and other types of questions
- Using questions to be in control while never being perceived as being controlling
- Strategic listening (listening for content and emotion, as well as what's not being said)
- Finding the fog (listening for confusion, uncertainty and the absence of a confident path forward)
- Syncing Up™, speaking their language and developing authentic rapport
- Advanced calibration skills to read cues and reactions to you, what you are communicating and the experience they are having

- Speaking the language of benefits, optimally framing and positioning advantages and capabilities
- Positioning, framing and reframing to better manage focus and meaning
- Using vocal quality (tone, tempo, volume, strategic pauses) to both Sync Up™ and better manage meaning
- Storytelling, use of metaphor and analogy
- Focusing on the facilitation of a collaboration as opposed to delivering a sales pitch
- Always being conscious and effective in guiding the person to the next steps (the chess game of thinking multiple moves ahead and skillfully guiding the conversation on that path)
- Working through resistance and challenges while managing tension and trust
- When and how to appropriately "step into the emotion you detect, not over it"
- Adding value to the sales experience for the customer while positioning you and your organization to be ETDBW

All of these and more can be addressed through our Customized 4U approach. We invite you to contact us to learn more.

www.success-sciences.com/customized4u-our-story/

We hope this Microbook has provided you with a few new insights on how to enhance your success and look forward to being in conversation with you soon about your team and any needs related to Earning and Retaining MORE Successful Customer Relationships.

Success Sciences, Inc.

www.success-sciences.com

(813) 989-9900